HAPPY EASTER ACTIVITY BOOK

101 Activities:
Mazes, Word Search, Color-by-Number, Jokes, Dot-to-Dot, Seek-and-Find, Word Puzzles, How-to-Draw, Coloring Pages + More!
For Kids Ages 4-10

This book belongs to
_____

Dandelion
Creating opportunities for moments of
fun, learning, relaxation, and togetherness.
© 2022 Mt. Washington, KY, USA

Easter Word Search

Find and cross out all the listed words.
The words may go horizontally, vertically, diagonally, not backwards. Ignore spaces and dashes, if any.

```
P N F E P T C F G P
P L E R A C O L Q A
M X A S V S M O D R
E I C S T H T W Y A
S H R H T R Y E E D
P F O A I I Q R R E
R B N L C C C P H V
I O W I Y L K E O D
N W Q S L T E E G B
G D Q D R Y X K N G
```

BOW
CHICKEN
DYE
EASTER
FLOWER
HOLY
MIRACLE
NEST
PARADE
PLASTIC EGG
SPRING

BOUQUET
BUNNY
CARROT
CROSS
HEN
EASTER
HOP
LAMB
LENT
RISEN
BRUNCH

```
O S G C A R R O T C
D R I S E N M A W R
H B I Z K B S B B O
E X O S B R U R U S
L A G U G B S U N S
X I S L Q A R N N N
H I L T L U A C Y S
O O A F E I E H H C
P U M K N R S T E V
U W B C T E D I N N
```

See answer key page 104.

A-Maze-ing Easter Egg

Can you help the bunny find his way through the egg maze?

See answer key page 104.

Color by Number

Color the numbers using the color key below.

YELLOW	GREY	BLUE	RED	PINK	GREEN
1	2	3	4	5	6

Find the Match

Can you find two identical eggs?

See answer key page 104.

Easter Dot-To-Dot

Draw a line from dot number 1 to dot number 2, then from dot number 2 to dot number 3, 3 to 4, and so on. Continue to join the dots until you have all the numbered dots. Then color the picture!

See answer key page 104.

Easter CROSSWORD

Use the pictures as clues to complete the crossword.

See answer key page 104.

Dot-to-Dot

Draw a line from dot number 1 to dot number 2, then from dot number 2 to dot number 3, 3 to 4, and so on. Continue to join the dots until you have all the numbered dots. Then color the picture!

Easter Funnies

How can you make Easter preparations go faster?
Use the eggs-press lane!

What do you call an Easter egg from outer space?
An egg-straterrestrial!

See answer key page 104.

Find the Differences

Can you find all ten differences in the picture below? Circle them.

Can you find the two identical chicks below? Circle them.

See answer key page 104.

Easter Word Scramble

Unscramble the letters of these Easter words.

BNYNU _____

COTRAR _____

ESATER _____

YED _____

OHP _____

DNAYC _____

MLAB _____

ADRBE _____

OWELFR _____

BSDRI _____

OQUUBET _____

ITSCLPA GEG _____

GSINPR _____

LKDCGUIN _____

See answer key page 104.

A-Maze-ing Eggs

Help the pencils find the way to the middle of the maze to color the eggs.

See answer key page 104.

How many words can you make from the letters in

Happy Easter

1. _____
2. _____
3. _____
4. _____
5. _____
6. _____
7. _____
8. _____
9. _____
10. _____
11. _____
12. _____
13. _____
14. _____
15. _____
16. _____
17. _____
18. _____
19. _____
20. _____
21. _____
22. _____
23. _____
24. _____

See answer key page 104.

Zig-Zag Easter Word Search

Find and circle all the listed words. The words may go left, right, up, down, not diagonally, and can bend at a right angle. There are no unused letters in the grid, every letter is used only once.

C	H	O	C	P	A	I	N	T	E
T	A	L	O	C	S	G	G	E	D
E	N	U	S	H	I	C	K	S	B
B	D	A	Y	H	P	A	L	M	O
U	R	E	E	O	L	I	E	F	N
N	G	I	T	Y	A	D	G	R	N
N	T	N	T	N	U	H	G	O	E
Y	E	G	C	A	R	D	S	N	T
S	K	S	A	B	R	E	T	D	H
P	R	I	N	G	E	A	S	T	A

BONNIE HAT
CHICKS
CHOCOLATE BUNNY
EASTER BASKET
PALM FROND
SPRING
SUNDAY
EGG HUNT
GREETING CARDS
~~HOLIDAY~~
PAINTED EGGS

See answer key page 105.

Easter Crossword

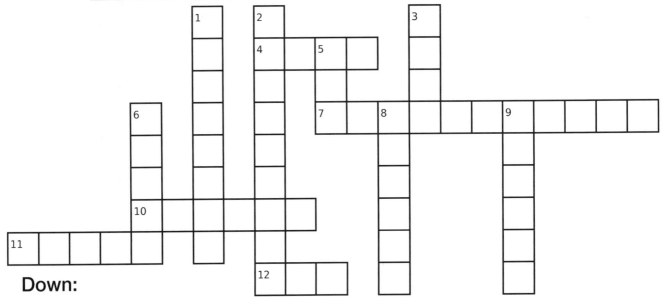

Down:

1. a baby duck
2. _____ eggs are sweet on Easter
3. where a bird lays eggs
5. we do this to eggs before Easter
6. girls wear on Easter
8. season of Easter
9. used to collect eggs

Across:

4. we do this to eggs on Easter
7. brings children treats on Easter
10. day Easter falls on
11. An Easter candy made from marshmallow
12. hidden on Easter

EASTER I SPY

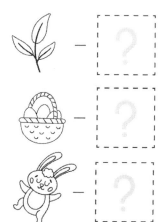

Copy the Picture

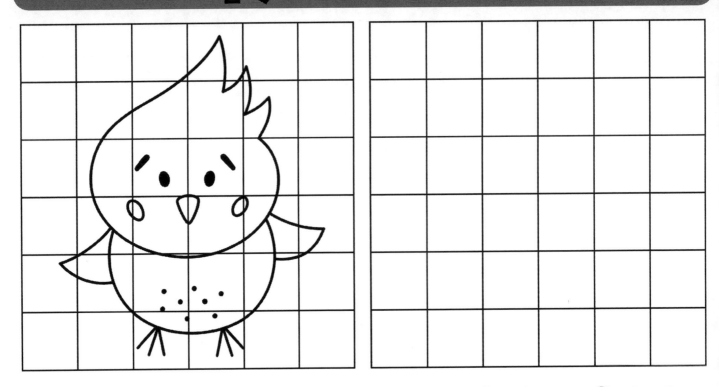

Can you find 10 differences between the two pictures?

30 See answer key page 105.

Mirrored Images

Can you find the mirrored copy for every picture?

See answer key page 105.

Draw an Easter Bunny

Use the guided steps to draw a bunny in the box below.

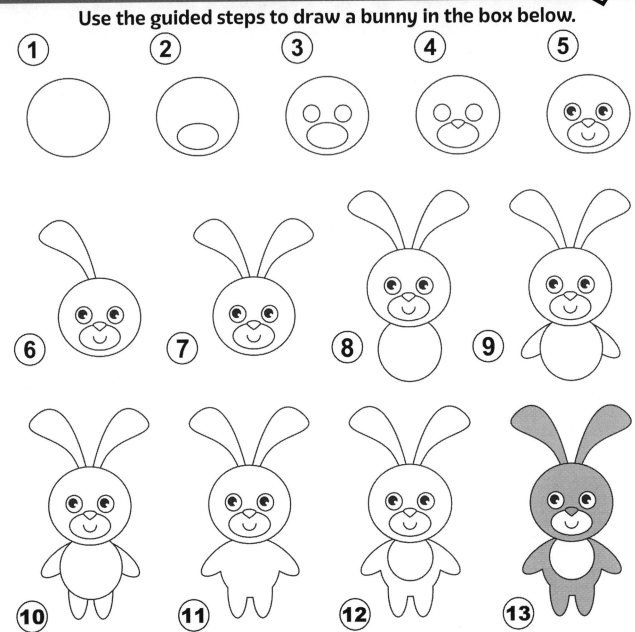

HAPPY EASTER!
Word Search

Find and circle all the listed words. The words may go left, right, up, down, not diagonally, and can bend at a right angle.

B	E	C	H	I	C	K	E
U	B	G	R	N	W	C	N
T	U	N	N	Y	A	T	T
T	K	C	Y	F	F	L	O
E	A	K	U	H	B	Y	W
R	F	L	Y	E	N	E	E
Y	K	E	T	C	R	G	R
C	A	R	R	O	T	G	E

- BABIES
- BLOOM
- LADYBUG
- FLOWERS
- GREEN
- IRIS
- NATURE
- HONEY BEE
- RAINBOW
- THAW
- TULIP

See answer key page 105.

How many words can you make from the letters in CHOCOLATE BUNNY

1. _____
2. _____
3. _____
4. _____
5. _____
6. _____
7. _____
8. _____
9. _____
10. _____
11. _____
12. _____
13. _____
14. _____
15. _____
16. _____
17. _____
18. _____
19. _____
20. _____
21. _____
22. _____
23. _____
24. _____
25. _____
26. _____

See answer key page 105.

What kind of bunny can't hop?
A chocolate bunny.

A-Maze-ing Egg

Can you find the way through the egg maze?

See answer key page 105.

Color by Number

Color the numbers using the key below to discover the hidden picture.

YELLOW	LIGHT GREY	BROWN	BLACK	PINK	GREEN	RED	BLUE
1	2	3	4	5	6	7	8

Easter Laughs

Why did the Easter Bunny have to fire the duck?
Because he kept quacking the eggs!

What's the best way to make Easter easier?
Put an "i" where the "t" is.

FIND THE SHADOW
Match each bunny to its shadow.

FIND THE DIFFERENCES
Can you find 5 differences between the two pictures?

See answer key page 105.

A-Maze-ing Egg

Can you find the way through the egg maze?

See answer key page 105.

Hilarious Easter Jokes

Share these Easter funnies with your family and friends!

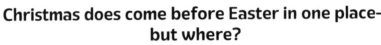

What do you call a rabbit with fleas?
Bugs Bunny.

Christmas does come before Easter in one place— but where?
The dictionary!

What happened to the Easter Bunny when he misbehaved at school?
He was eggspelled!

How does the Easter Bunny stay in shape?
He eggs-ercises.

What did the Easter Bunny say to the carrot?
Nice gnawing you.

Why does the Easter Bunny want to win a gold medal?
Because he heard it's 24 carrot.

How does an Easter Bunny keep his fur looking so good?
Hare spray.

What happened when the Easter Bunny met the rabbit of his dreams?
They lived hoppily ever after!

What do you call a rabbit that tells good jokes?
A funny bunny.

What did the Easter Bunny say to the carrot?
Nice gnawing you.

Why did the Easter Bunny have on a hat?
Because he was having a bad hare day.

What do you call a rabbit with the sniffles?
A runny bunny.

What is the Easter Bunny's favorite dance?
The bunny hop.

What is Easter Bunny's favorite kind of music?
Hip-hop!

What did the Easter Bunny do after its wedding?
Went on a nice bunnymoon.

How can you tell which rabbits are the oldest in a group?
Just look for the gray hares.

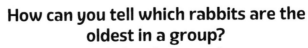

A-Maze-ing Egg

Can you find the way through the egg maze?

See answer key page 106.

Color by Number

Color the numbers using the key below.

| LIGHT BLUE 1 | YELLOW 2 | PINK 3 | ORANGE 4 |

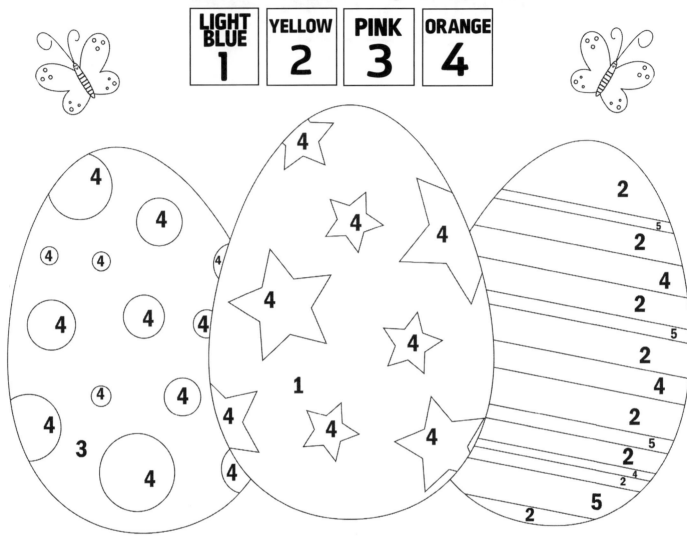

Easter Funnies

Where does Easter take place every year?
Where eggs marks the spot!

Where does the Easter Bunny get his eggs?
From an eggplant.

What do you call a very tired Easter egg?
Eggs-austed

Why can't a rabbit's nose be 12 inches long?
Because then it would be a foot!

What should you do to prepare for all the Easter treats?
Eggs-ercise!

Dot-to-Dot

Draw a line from dot number 1 to dot number 2, then from dot number 2 to dot number 3, 3 to 4, and so on. Continue to join the dots until you have all the numbered dots. Then color the picture!

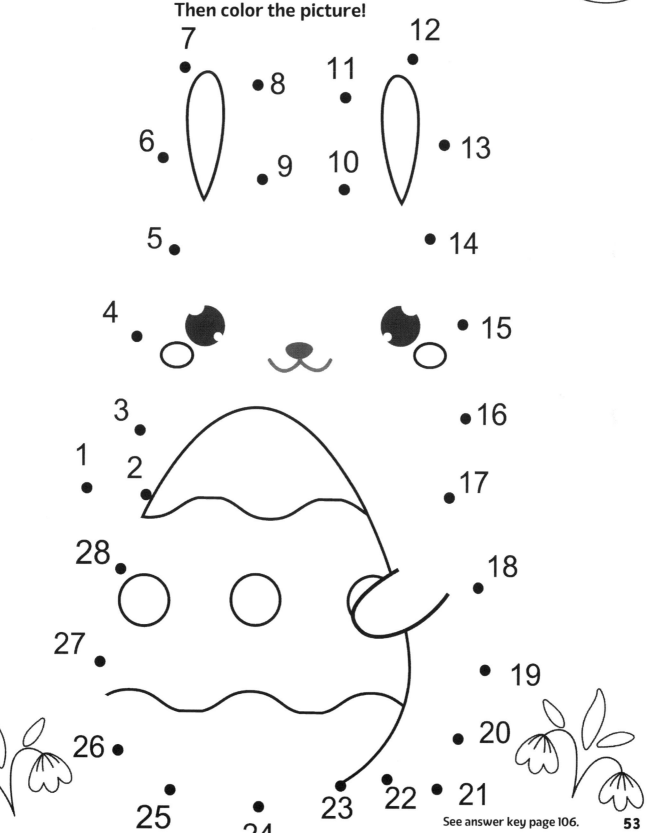

See answer key page 106.

Find the Differences
Can you find 10 differences between the two pictures?

There is one flower with five petals. **Find this flower.**

Bunny's Maze

Can you help bunny find his way through the maze to the carrot?

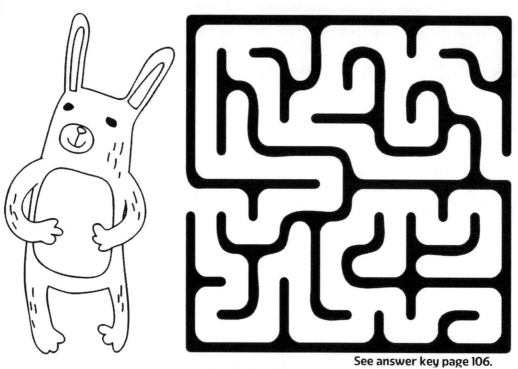

See answer key page 106.

Xs and Os

Color by Number

Color the numbers using the key below to discover the hidden picture.

YELLOW	BROWN	ORANGE	PINK	LIGHT BLUE	GREEN
1	2	3	4	5	6

Can you find 10 differences between the two pictures?

FIND THE MATCHING SHADOW

See answer key page 106.

Dot-to-Dot

Draw a line from dot number 1 to dot number 2, then from dot number 2 to dot number 3, 3 to 4, and so on. Continue to join the dots until you have all the numbered dots. Then color the picture!

See answer key page 106.

Easter Word Search

Find and circle all the listed words. The words may go horizontally, vertically, diagonally, not backwards.

```
                        H M U
                        C C M X Y
                        X R E L O
                        O U A H Q
            B B T       F H S I C         N Y D
D Y X R W   P C T F L           W H I T E
O E M F E Y   V E P       C K H G X I
J H C K P A F Y R A B U K D C O Y
V S O S O D B B T E D D G J D
    E J R V N J U T A U T A D
        A T K N E L C
        H S L T Q N R E K G X
        P E A C E E Y N M L N E F
    X O B M A B     J   D I M L B M
    W Y P P A H     O   S N V B T H
    L R C Y H       Y       G H I D
        Q W Z       Z       E B K
                    Y
                    Z
                    Y
                    E
                    L
                    L
                    O
                    W
                    E
                    G
                    G

        S S O C H O C O L A T E E G G
        G I B S M N A Q Z Y S J F O F
        A M U E A P D Y Z M C O F
        J Q X T Z X M H P E T Y R
        H P R O T P B P G L I W J
        D G O V J E N I X C C F H
        S E A S T E R S U N D A Y
        Y I P S V S F S H A B
        E R Y U Z O R L V M K
        A Z N L I R H K Y Y O
        T W D K O M W R Q
```

BUTTERFLY
CHOCOLATE EGG
CHURCH
DECORATE
DUCKLING
EASTER BUNNY
EASTER SUNDAY
HAPPY
OVAL
PATTERN
PEACE
WHITE
YELLOW EGG
BIBLE
BREAD

See answer key page 106.

Draw a Chick

Use the guided steps to draw a chick in the box below.

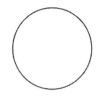
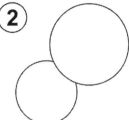
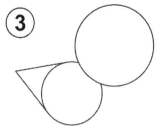
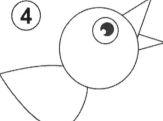

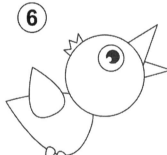

Draw an Easter Basket

Use the guided steps to draw an Easter basket in the box below.

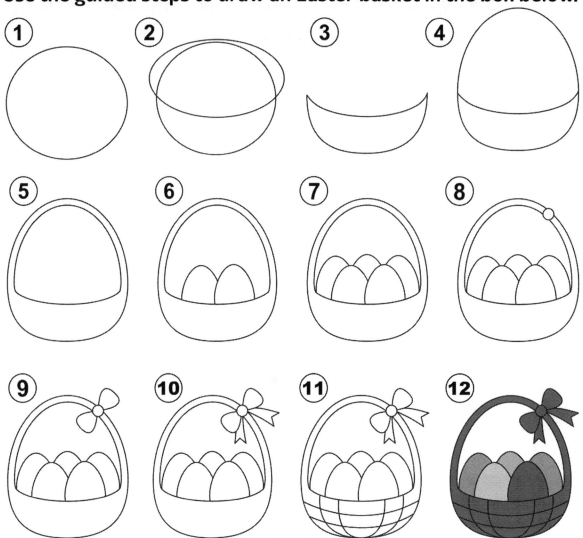

Finish the Picture

Use the grid as your guide to finish the Easter bunny picture in the bottom square.

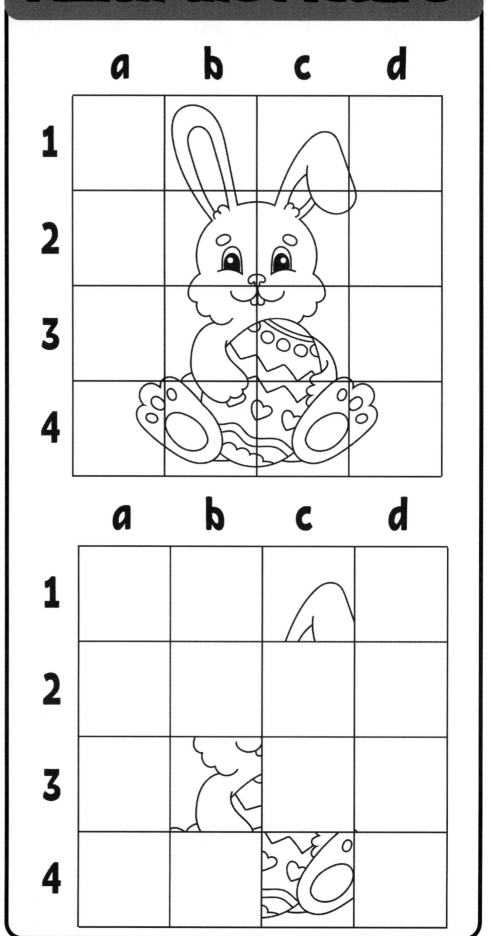

Egg Hunt Word Search

Find and circle all the listed words. The words may go horizontally, vertically, diagonally, not backwards.

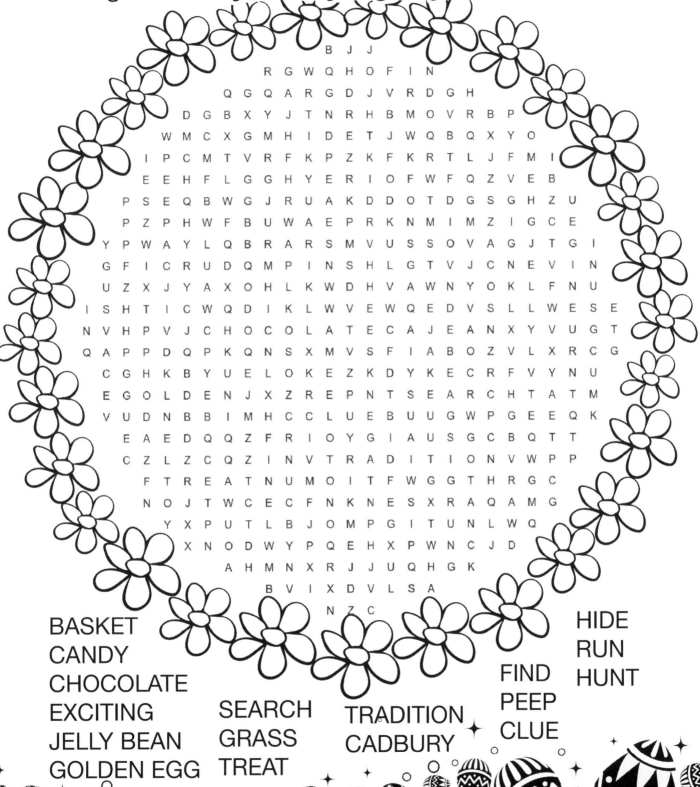

BASKET
CANDY
CHOCOLATE
EXCITING
JELLY BEAN
GOLDEN EGG
SEARCH
GRASS
TREAT
TRADITION
CADBURY
HIDE
RUN
HUNT
FIND
PEEP
CLUE

An A-Maze-ing Egg

Can you find the way through the egg maze?

76   See answer key page 107.

Can you find 8 differences between the two pictures?

See answer key page 107.

Easter Funnies

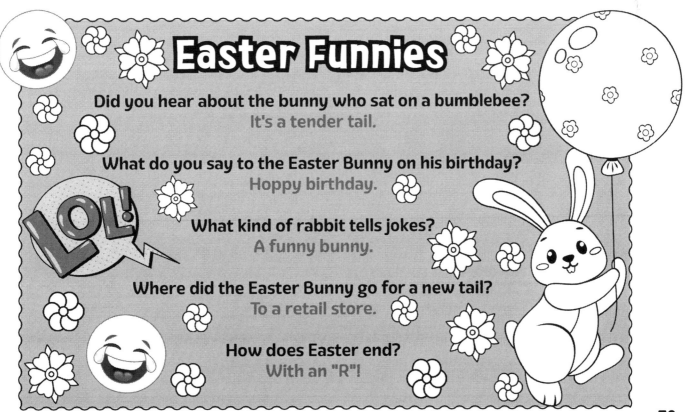

Did you hear about the bunny who sat on a bumblebee?
It's a tender tail.

What do you say to the Easter Bunny on his birthday?
Hoppy birthday.

What kind of rabbit tells jokes?
A funny bunny.

Where did the Easter Bunny go for a new tail?
To a retail store.

How does Easter end?
With an "R"!

How many words can you make from the letters in

EGG BASKET

1. _____
2. _____
3. _____
4. _____
5. _____
6. _____
7. _____
8. _____
9. _____
10. _____
11. _____
12. _____
13. _____
14. _____
15. _____
16. _____
17. _____
18. _____
19. _____
20. _____
21. _____
22. _____
23. _____
24. _____
25. _____
26. _____
27. _____
28. _____
29. _____
30. _____
31. _____
32. _____
33. _____

See answer key page 107.

Can you find 10 differences between the two pictures?

Whose Nestling?

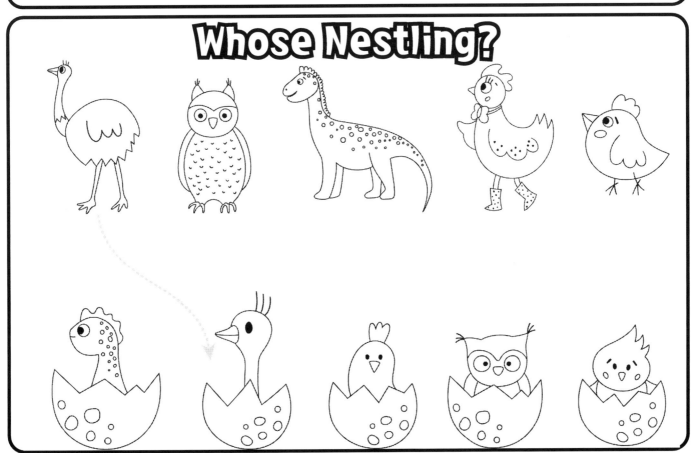

See answer key page 107.

Complete the Pictures

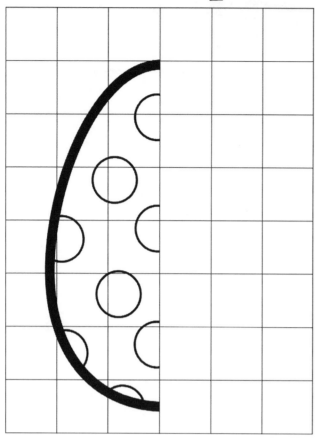
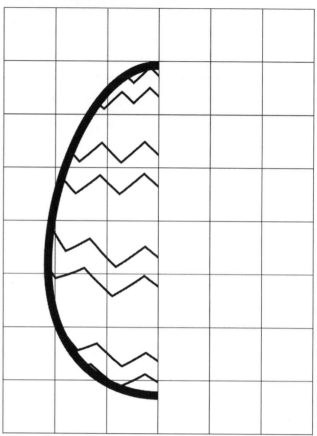
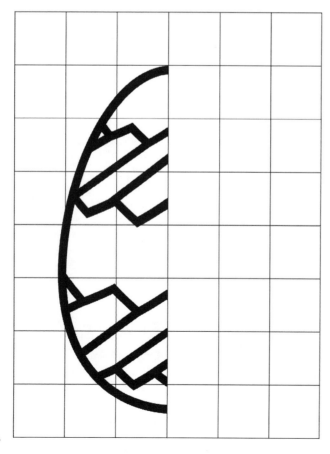
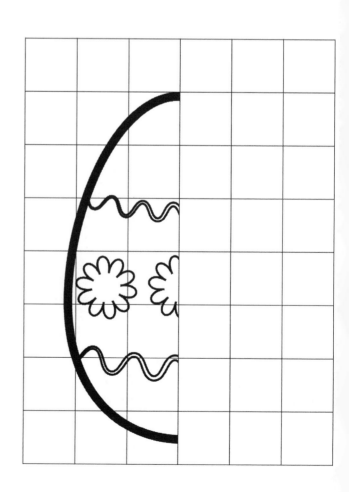

An A-Mazeing Egg

Can you find the way through the egg maze?

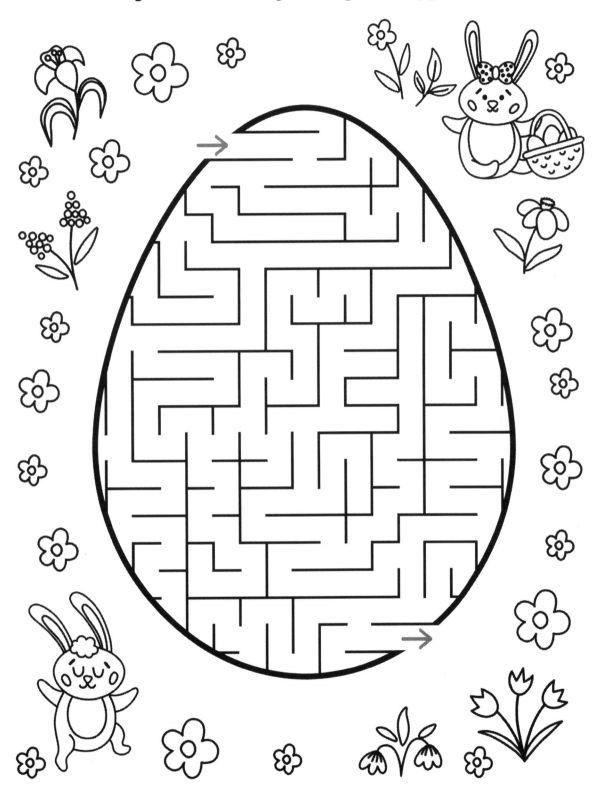

See answer key page 107. **87**

Dot-to-Dot

Draw a line from dot number 1 to dot number 2, then from dot number 2 to dot number 3, 3 to 4, and so on. Continue to join the dots until you have all the numbered dots. Then color the picture!

See answer key page 107.

Easter Funnies

What did the Easter bunny say about the Easter parade?
It was eggs-cellent.

What did the Easter egg ask for at the hair salon?
A new dye-job.

Can you find 10 differences between the two pictures?

Find two same objects.

See answer key page 107.

Find the Match
Can you find the two matching egg halves?

Easter Word Scramble

OCOEALTHC _____

GGE UHTN _____

ASTEBK _____

LEYLJ ENBA _____

See answer key page 107.

Egg Match

Can you find the match for each card?

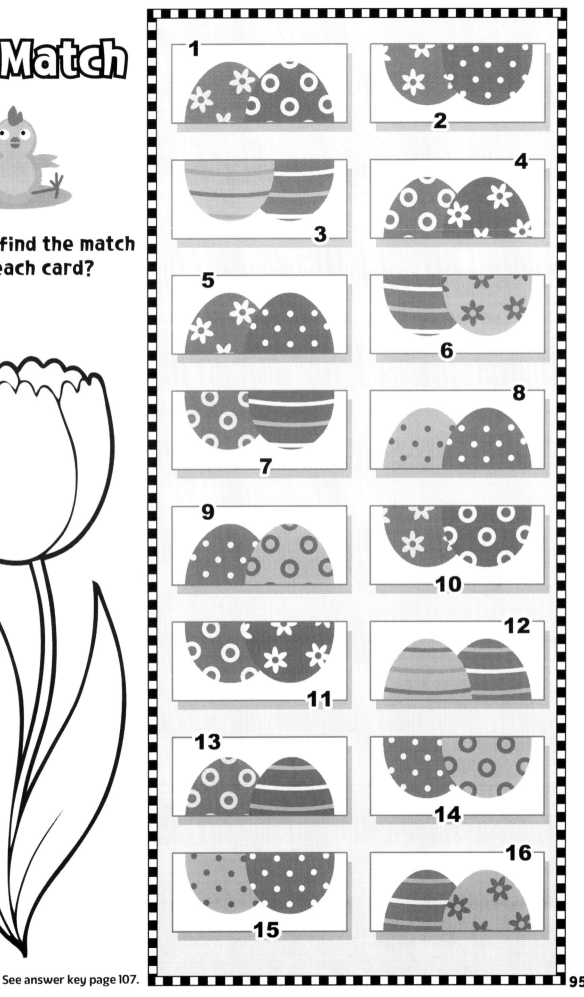

Easter Maze

Can you help the bunny find the way to the Easter basket?

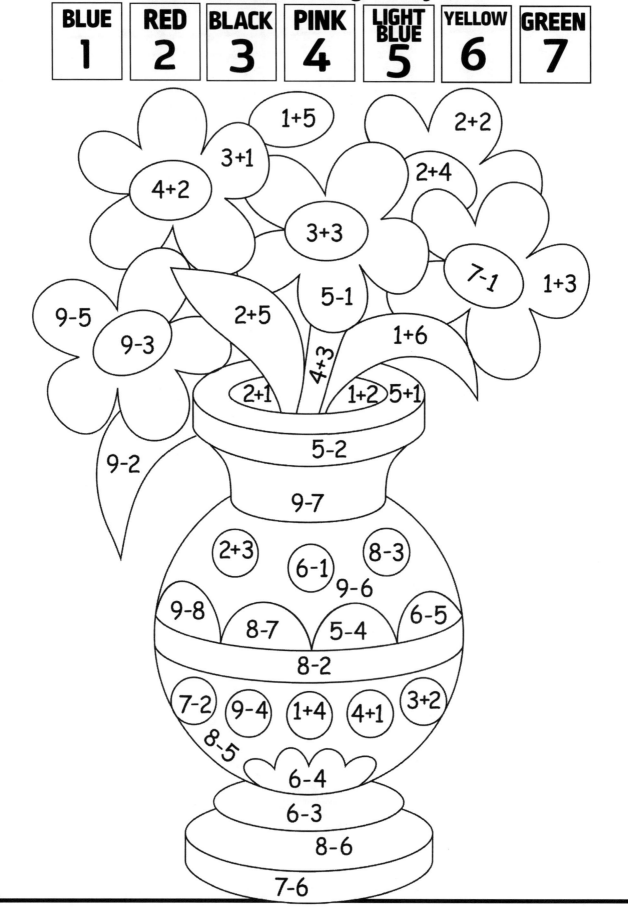

Shadow Match

Match each picture to the correct shadow.

See answer key page 107.

Dot-to-Dot

Draw a line from dot number 1 to dot number 2, then from dot number 2 to dot number 3, 3 to 4, and so on. Continue to join the dots until you have all the numbered dots. Then color the picture!

See answer key page 107.

Easter Egg Maze

Can you help the pencils find their way out of the maze to color the eggs?

Activity Answers

Pg. 2

P	N	F	E	P	T	C	F	G	P
P	L	E	R	A	C	O	L	Q	A
M	X	A	S	V	S	M	O	F	R
E	I	C	S	T	H	T	W	Y	A
S	H	R	H	T	R	Y	E	E	D
P	F	O	A	I	I	Q	R	R	E
R	B	N	L	C	C	C	P	H	V
I	O	W	I	Y	L	K	E	O	D
N	W	Q	S	L	T	E	E	G	B
G	D	Q	D	R	Y	X	K	N	G

O	S	G	C	A	R	R	O	T	C
D	R	I	S	E	N	M	A	W	R
H	B	I	Z	K	B	S	B	R	O
E	X	O	S	B	R	U	R	U	S
L	A	G	U	G	B	S	U	N	S
X	I	S	L	Q	A	R	N	C	N
H	O	I	L	T	L	U	C	H	C
O	O	A	M	F	E	I	H	E	V
P	U	M	F	K	N	R	S	E	N
U	W	B	C	T	E	D	I	N	

Pg. 4

Pg. 6
6, 18

Pg. 9

Pg. 10
1. Butterfly
2. Carrot
3. Chicken
4. Hen
5. Flower
6. Bunny
7. Egg

Pg. 13
Easter Word Puzzle:
Happy Easter, Stop and Smell the Flowers

Pg. 14

Pg. 17

Pg. 21

Pg. 22
HAPPY EASTER

he	hay	see	yet	hats	party
hey	sat	sea	yes	apes	trash
spy	say	try	arts	peep	traps
ape	pay	say	eyes	type	earth
art	she	yet	hats	tree	three
her	pea	are	peer	star	paste
hat	set	ash	pest	tear	years
tap	pet	tee	pets	rest	share
				pasta	sheet
				spray	artsy
				happy	hearts

Pg. 18

BNYNU	BUNNY
COTRAR	CARROT
ESATER	EASTER
YED	DYE
OHP	HOP
DNAYC	CANDY
MLAB	LAMB
ADRBE	BREAD
OWELFR	FLOWER
BSDRI	BIRDS
OQUUBET	BOUQUET
ITSCLPA GEG	PLASTIC EGG
GSINPR	SPRING
LKDCGUIN	DUCKLING

Pg. 25

Pg. 26

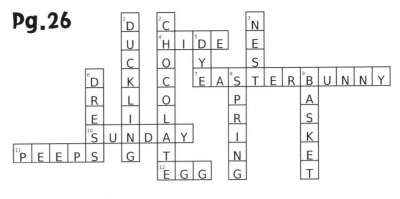

Pg. 29

butterfly – 7, leaf – 8, mouse – 6
egg – 9, basket – 2, flowers – 4
chick – 5, bunny – 1, chicken – 3

Pg. 30

Pg. 33

1–4, 2–9, 3–10, 5–7, 6–11, 8–12

Pg. 37

B	E	C	H	I	C	K	E
U	B	G	R	N	W	C	N
T	U	N	N	Y	A	T	T
T	K	C	Y	F	F	L	O
E	A	K	U	H	B	Y	W
R	F	L	Y	E	N	E	E
Y	K	E	T	C	R	G	R
C	A	R	R	O	T	G	E

Pg. 38 CHOCOLATE BUNNY

he	act	ten	chat	cable
to	yet	boy	cane	teach
no	you	but	boot	bathe
an	ace	can	cent	batch
be	bat	cat	clan	alone
at	ban	tan	then	beach
hen	ate	holy	ouch	nacho
toe	any	heal	noon	cocoa
lot	ant	heat	neon	ocean
toy	one	each	than	beauty
ton	out	lane	only	toucan
hey	bye	hoot	catch	chance
bay	buy	can't	clean	coyote
yea	the	cute	canoe	

Pg. 40

Pg. 43

Pg. 44

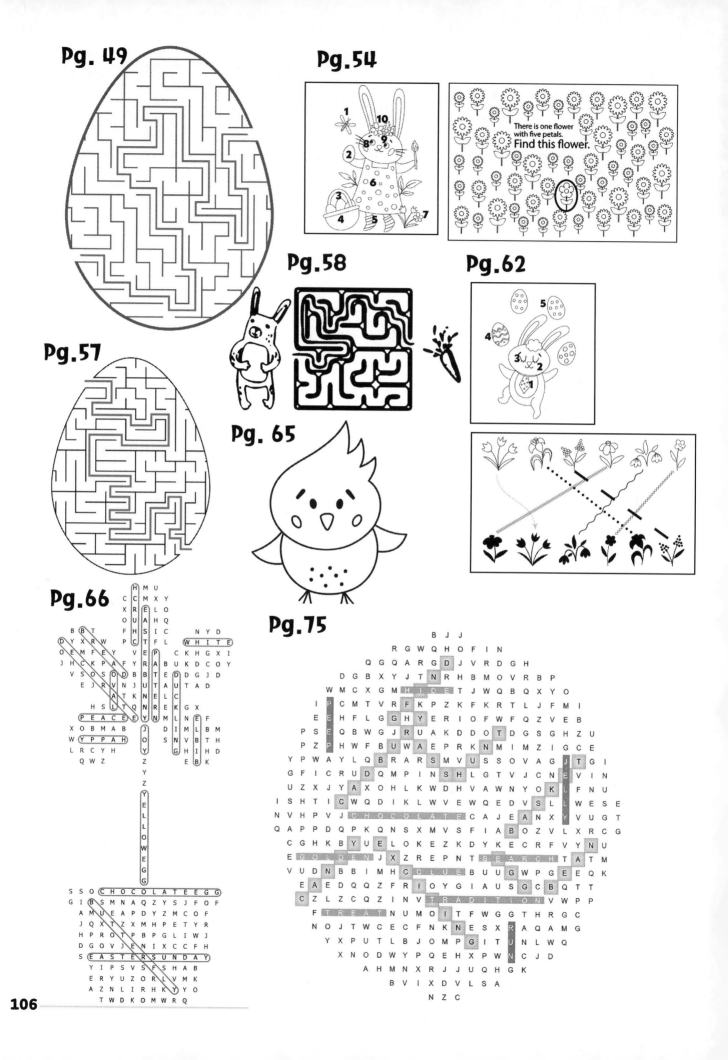

Pg.76

Pg79

Pg.80
EGG BASKET
Be	tea	bees	sage
at	age	bats	skate
sat	bag	beat	stage
set	eat	east	bakes
get	egg	best	beast
bat	bee	bets	gates
tee	beg	beak	beets
tag	bake	seek	geeks
ask	eats	gate	basket
ate	beet	teas	

Pg.83

Pg.83
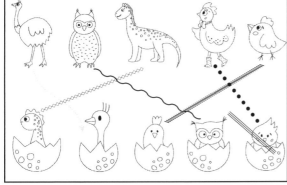

Pg.87

Pg.88

Pg.91

Pg.92
OCOEALTHC CHOCOLATE
GGE UHTN   EGG HUNT
ASTEBK   BASKET
LEYLJ ENBA JELLY BEAN

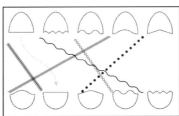

Pg.95
1–10, 2–5,
3–12, 4–11
6–16, 7–13,
8–15, 9–14

Pg.96
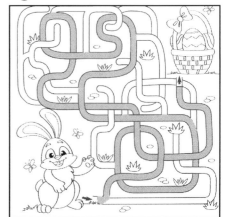

Pg.103

Pg.100

Pg.99
1–8, 3–4, 5–12,
7–6 9–10, 11–2

More from Dandelion

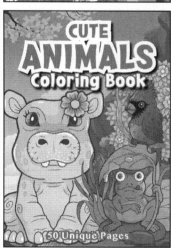

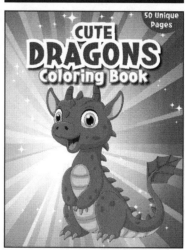

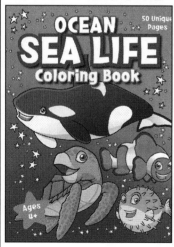
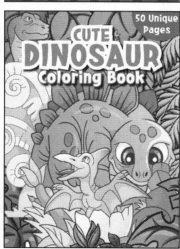
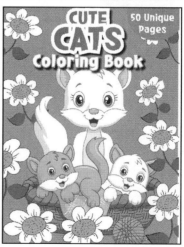
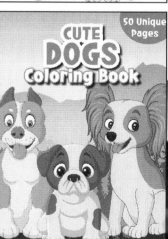

THANK YOU SO MUCH FOR PURCHASING THIS BOOK!

We would sure appreciate it if you would take a minute to let us know what you think by leaving a review on Amazon.com.

This small act goes a long way to helping our small independent publishing business make the best books possible and reach more great people like you.

Made in United States
Orlando, FL
26 March 2024

45164234R00061